SPOOKY NIGHTMARES

CONTENTS

SPOOKY CIRCUS TRAIN

Timmy is an ordinary boy who adores scary things. He is on a wild ride through the realm of nightmares. "Whooooo wants to see the greatest show in Nightmare Land?" Timmy's nightmare starts with an unusual circus train. The engine is decorated with bones, and the clowns are all skeletons! Usually a place for laughs and cheers, the circus can be very spooky in the land of bad dreams.

ALL ABOARD!

If you have some LEGO® train wheel bases, use them to build a circus train for a nightmare carnival. Make an engine in front and a car for it to pull. Inside could be snakes, spiders, or something even scarier!

COME ONE, COME ALL, TO THE NIGHTMARE CARNIVAL!

Build a hollow box for the freight car

Turn plates sideways to build letters. Pick a color that will stand out against the background

If you don't have this "cow catcher" piece, build one out of slope bricks

WE ONLY RUN A SKELETON SERVICE.

White robot arms create ribcage-like decorations on the engine's sides

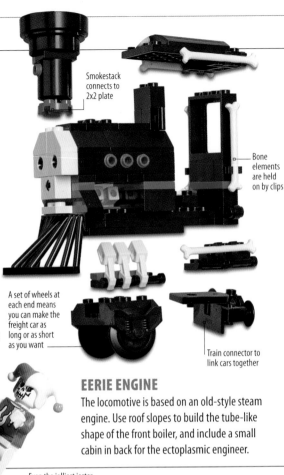

Smokestack connects to 2x2 plate

Bone elements are held on by clips

A set of wheels at each end means you can make the freight car as long or as short as you want

Train connector to link cars together

EERIE ENGINE

The locomotive is based on an old-style steam engine. Use roof slopes to build the tube-like shape of the front boiler, and include a small cabin in back for the ectoplasmic engineer.

Even the jolliest jester looks creepy with a skeleton head

Blue LEGO Technic half-pins provide detail

The skull has LEGO Technic bricks-with-holes for eye sockets and a brick with a cross-axle hole for its nose

FRONT VIEW

FORTUNE TELLER

In the land of nightmares, fortune tellers never warn you about tomorrow's surprise math test. Mix and match minifigure parts and accessories to populate your carnival with colorful performers and other odd characters.

I SEE NICE THINGS IN YOUR FUTURE.

NO! I LIKE HORRIBLE THINGS!

Crystal ball is a transparent minifigure head piece under a transparent 2x2 hollow dome

Bell is a 1x1 round plate and a 2x2 round brick attached to a radar dish with a printed swirl

GAME OF STRENGTH

You don't have to add bone details to this test-your-strength game to make it spooky. Just build it out of clashing colors and give it a scary attendant—it will fit right in with your nightmare carnival!

Use a tooth plate to mark the strongest swing

Build the game as a long, thin base with a short wall at one end, and then flip it up

Hammer is a long bar, a brick with a hollow side stud, two 1x1 plates, and a 1x1 tile

NIGHTMARE CARNIVAL

"Last stop! Everybody off!" The carnival is a maze of games, rides, and snack booths, each with its own scary twist. Timmy likes cotton candy, but he is pretty sure he doesn't want to try the rotten candy that they're selling here! Build fiendishly fun rides and attractions to give visitors to your nightmare carnival a good scare.

Make sure the tunnel arches are high enough for the car and passengers to roll through

A spider in a web makes any scene look extra-spooky!

ENTRANCE VIEW

GHOSTLY RIDE

You don't have to build the entire carnival ride—just a stretch of track and a haunted interior. Build spooky details into the wall that will make the riders jump in their seats!

Sign is a sideways wall of stacked green and black bricks and plates

Add plants, cats, bats, and fro to bring your scary ride to life

Use textured bricks in the back wall to make it look old and decrepit

Old-fashioned lamps are four-forked palm tree tops with transparent 1x1 round plates inside, and a small radar dish as a lid

Lock pieces together well so the arches don't fall apart

I WANT MY MOMMY!

ON TARGET

Use printed tiles and microfigures from LEGO® Games as targets for a carnival shooting game. Hit one and you will get a prize... but are you sure you want whatever it is that you'll win?

IF YOU MISS, YOU HAVE TO SIT ON THE SHELF.

Make a striped awning with arch pieces in alternating colors

Crossbow handles are plugged into jumper plates

Use stacked-up log bricks or 1x2 brown bricks to make the stall's wooden sides

CRAZY CAR

Use a pair of train wheel bases to make a small ride car. A 2x6 hollow space on top is just the right size for three frightened minifigures to sit inside. Build your car in a color that stands out against the wall's dark background.

Where will your ghost train go next? Will there be more track, or a sheer drop?

Car is symmetrical front-to-back so it can roll either way

Headlight is a 1x1 transparent yellow round plate

Bumpers are sideways-built curved bars with studs attached to headlight bricks

HAUNTED HOUSE

Next, Timmy dreams about a house where monsters live. It has all kinds of creepy rooms and an attic full of specters! A haunted house is more than just a brick building with creatures placed inside. Think about what kinds of rooms your monsters would like, and don't forget the most important part of the model: the ghosts!

Black fence pieces look like a foreboding iron railing

Mix round and square plates in different colors to make a low stone wall

FRONT VIEW

Sprinkle in some dark gray bricks for an old stone building

Build bricks with side studs into the walls to attach vines and ivy to the outside

Get your teeth into this Vampire Car build on p.10!

SIDE VIEW

Blood-red rooftops add to the haunted ambience

Spider web attaches to a bar mounted on clips in the wall

A LEGO Technic brick creates a hole for bats to fly in and out!

6

UP-SCARES, DOWN-SCARES

This model is half house and half castle, full of musty old history. Inside are cavernous chambers with arches and alcoves that could hide all manner of scary things. It is built in two halves—each half is connected by 1x2 hinge bricks so it can swing open, revealing the shadowy, haunted interior.

A pair of plates with handles becomes a gothic carved windowsill

1x1 round plate

2x2 round brick

2x2 round tile with clock pattern

TIME PIECE

It won't take a long time to build this clock! A printed round tile is used for the clock face and a minifigure wrench for the pendulum.

Use an arch or build a column in the middle of the open side to support the roof bricks overhead

Why not extend your haunted house? Fill it with more rooms full of spooky stuff to scare visitors!

Upper story lifts off, making it easier to access the study

BOO!

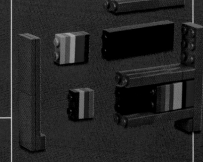

HELLO! IT MUST BE TIME FOR SUPPER!

THE MASTER'S LAIR

The cultured Count has his own library and study in the main downstairs chamber. His prized bookcase is built sideways, with stacks of colored 1x2 plates as books on the shelves.

Jumper plates in the tile floorboards connect animals and objects

MONSTER MOTORS

What is that terrifying growling sound? Is it a werewolf? A dinosaur? No—it's a crazy custom car with a monster at the wheel! Build a pint-sized auto to fit your favorite LEGO monster minifigure. Give it a design and color scheme that reflects what kind of creature drives it, and roll it around to wreak some havoc!

This engine piece can be found in many LEGO vehicle sets

Bricks with side studs and half-arch bricks at the front of the car allow you to attach a sideways-built bumper

FRONT VIEW

> IF I GET A FLAT TIRE, I USE A PUMPKIN PATCH!

Curved elements mimic a pumpkin's shape

Big exposed wheels and engine capture the look of a classic hot rod racer

PUMPKIN CAR

What could be a better ride for a pumpkin-headed monster than a pumpkin-themed car? With its bright orange color scheme and rounded curves, this model definitely shows its jack-o'-lantern influence.

> CAR NO WORK. FRANKIE USE HIS BOLTS.

FRONT VIEW

MONSTER CAR

Use pieces that resemble wood, aluminum, and brass to build a chugging, puffing steampunk roadster fit for a makeshift monster assembled by mad science! Try combining your more unusual pieces to create even more unusual shapes.

Stack two plates with handles for a double bumper

Ray guns attach to silver telescopes held on by clips

STEAM POWER

The engine is built with a mix of metallic-colored elements. Gold robot arms and cones plugged onto silver ray gun handles give it six smokestacks for venting heat and steam.

Gold robot arms

Wagon wheels look rickety and old-fashioned

ESTER JET

...ou can use the same building techniques ...at you would use to make a mini monster ...r to build a haunted plane! Use arches, ...es, and sideways building to make its ...rface smooth and aerodynamic.

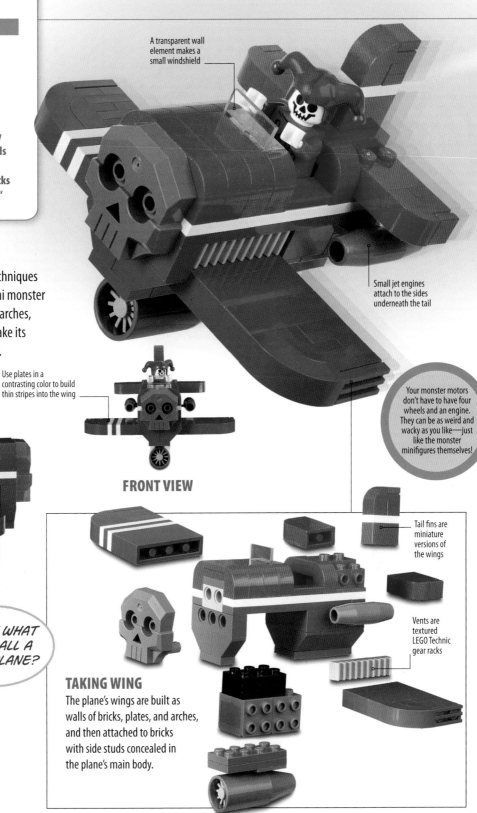

A transparent wall element makes a small windshield

Small jet engines attach to the sides underneath the tail

Use plates in a contrasting color to build thin stripes into the wing

Your monster motors don't have to have four wheels and an engine. They can be as weird and wacky as you like—just like the monster minifigures themselves!

FRONT VIEW

...erted slopes make ...underside look ...re rounded

SIDE VIEW

Tail fins are miniature versions of the wings

Vents are textured LEGO Technic gear racks

TAKING WING

The plane's wings are built as walls of bricks, plates, and arches, and then attached to bricks with side studs concealed in the plane's main body.

IS THAT WHAT THEY CALL A SCAREPLANE?

MONSTER RACE

Scary racers, start your engines! Timmy has no idea how he hs ended up as a referee for this race—as the racers career down the track, he realizes that he has no idea what the rules are, either! Build more monster cars to add to your monster collection—which one do you think would win in a monster race?

Headlights are unnecessary when the driver can see in the dark!

A 2x3 curved plate with hole creates a tombstone-like decoration

FRONT VIEW

GETTING STUCK IN TRAFFIC DRIVES ME BATTY!

Use a grille and two grille slopes to make a ribbed bumper

VAMPIRE CAR

Vampires are associated with the color black, bats, and coffins. That's why this model reflects all three! Roof slopes give the car the long, angular shape of a coffin, and the curved fins on the back are reminiscent of a bat's sweeping wings.

Close-fitting mudgu around the wheels p a sleek silhouette

Plates with handles add side details

Neon green bulbs make the engine look like it's powered by swamp water!

A textured brick makes a good small car grille

Use slope bricks to make angled surfaces

FRONT VIEW

SWAMP MONSTER CAR

Create a complementary color scheme by matching your car to the look of its driver. Can you tell that the swamp monster's favorite color is green? Transparent and bubble-like elements add to the auto's aquatic appearance.

Big tires for traction on marshy terrain

Match the details to the monster—build a skull-faced car for a skull-faced clown!

FRONT VIEW

CREEPY CLOWN CAR

What kind of color scheme should you give your custom car model? Clashing colors will really jump out and say "Boo!" to onlookers. If your driver has green hair, try a fiery red race car and add a yellow stripe to represent blazing speed!

An auto hood or roof piece also works well as a rear spoiler

★ **CHALLENGE**

Stack bricks in alternating colors to create checkered race markers

SCARY RACING

Challenge your friends to build their own monster mini-cars and race to become King or Queen of the Monsters. Build obstacles and ramps to make it super challenging—and super scary! Take turns giving your car a quick one-handed push and see who can reach the finish line first.

Build lots of ramps in different sizes

Nothing says "fast" like a giant plume of flame blasting out of the back of your vehicle!

ROCKET RACER

Use round pieces to build a jet engine, with a hole in the center for the flame element's peg. The front piece of the car is built with four curved macaroni bricks and matches the look of the red 4x4 round plate at the back.

Plug ray gun handles into bricks with hollow side studs to make angled engine exhaust pipes

A blue driver's seat makes this car's color scheme even more clashing!

Curved macaroni brick

Snap 1x1 round plates into the skull's eye sockets for eerie, staring headlights

4x4 round plate

DO YOU KNOW THE WAY TO THE BLOOD BANK?

SWEET DREAMS

"Phew, thank goodness that's over," Timmy says as he opens his eyes. But a sudden rattling tells him that he is still stuck in the nightmare! A bedroom is a place of safety and comfort. . .so where better to hide a spooky scare? Whether you build a skeleton in the closet or a monster under the bed, there won't be any sweet dreams here tonight!

Use printed or stickered tiles for wall decorations

A treasure chest can double as a trunk for storing clothes and toys

YIKES!

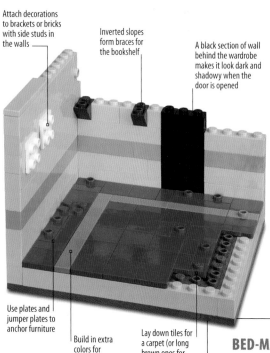

Attach decorations to brackets or bricks with side studs in the walls

Inverted slopes form braces for the bookshelf

A black section of wall behind the wardrobe makes it look dark and shadowy when the door is opened

Use plates and jumper plates to anchor furniture

Build in extra colors for wallpaper and rug designs

Lay down tiles for a carpet (or long brown ones for a wooden floor)

ROOM DESIGN

You can use this basic design to make lots of different kinds of rooms. It's just a floor and two walls, built up the normal way. The details and contents are up to you!

There's some space under the bed, so why not add a creature there?

BED-MAKING

Use plates to build the bed's frame and legs. Place small arches over the edges and fill in the center with tiles to make a patterned blanket or bed cover.

Lay a white tile across some jumper plates for the pillow

Include a plate to attach a sleeping minifigure or give a frightened one somewhere to stand

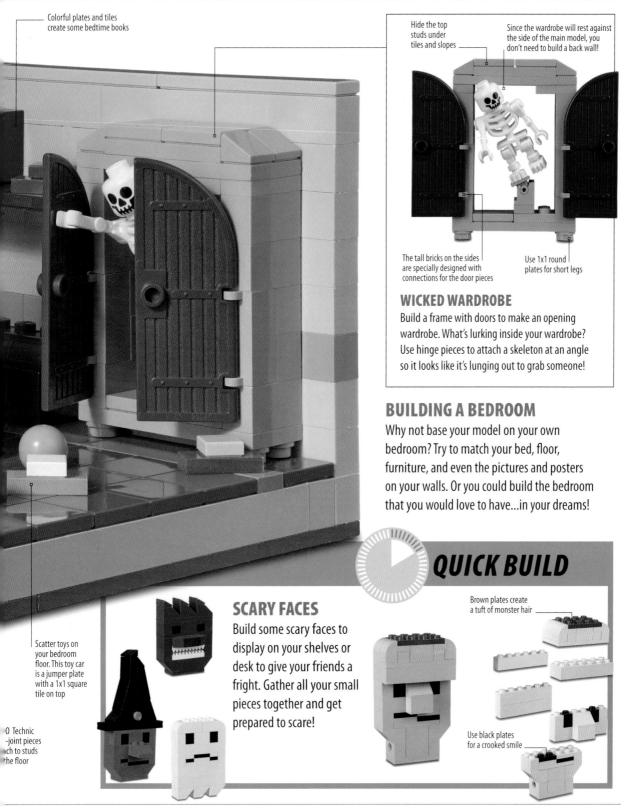

Colorful plates and tiles create some bedtime books

Hide the top studs under tiles and slopes

Since the wardrobe will rest against the side of the main model, you don't need to build a back wall!

The tall bricks on the sides are specially designed with connections for the door pieces

Use 1x1 round plates for short legs

WICKED WARDROBE

Build a frame with doors to make an opening wardrobe. What's lurking inside your wardrobe? Use hinge pieces to attach a skeleton at an angle so it looks like it's lunging out to grab someone!

BUILDING A BEDROOM

Why not base your model on your own bedroom? Try to match your bed, floor, furniture, and even the pictures and posters on your walls. Or you could build the bedroom that you would love to have...in your dreams!

QUICK BUILD

SCARY FACES

Build some scary faces to display on your shelves or desk to give your friends a fright. Gather all your small pieces together and get prepared to scare!

Brown plates create a tuft of monster hair

Use black plates for a crooked smile

Scatter toys on your bedroom floor. This toy car is a jumper plate with a 1x1 square tile on top

O Technic -joint pieces ch to studs he floor

SOMETHING IN THE BATH

Fleeing into the bathroom doesn't help Timmy. There are all kinds of strange noises in the plumbing…and what just made that splash?! An ordinary home can become an extraordinary one in the world of bad dreams. Bathrooms are just the start—think about what you can do to transform a kitchen or living room scene into some silly, scary fun!

Red and blue round plates on top of faucets show which is for hot water and which is for cold

Sink and bathtub are attached to the wall using bricks with side studs

A black nighttime background establishes the time and makes the monster stand out even more

LEGO® Alien Conquest head

BATHROOM NIGHTMARE

This bathroom is built in much the same way as the bedroom on p.12, but with different fixtures and furnishings. The familiar tub, sink, and toilet make it clear where in the house this particular scare is taking place!

BOO!

BOO HOO!

TENTACLES IN THE TUB

Use bricks with holes and side studs to build the bathtub. The creature under the water is built with tail elements plugged into the bricks. Attach the tub to the bathroom floor using plates and bricks with side studs.

Exposed studs make the red floor look like a deep-pile carpet

KNOCK KNOCK!

Mom, there's a monster outside! A spooky face in the window turns a simple home-life scene into the start of an alien invasion. Building it in a slightly larger scale makes the minifigure look like a small (and very scared) child.

White bricks for bubbles created by the bath beast!

Place arches on their sides to make rounded corners like a real bathtub

Bath water is a sideways wall of blue bricks

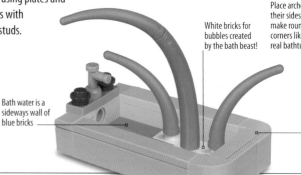

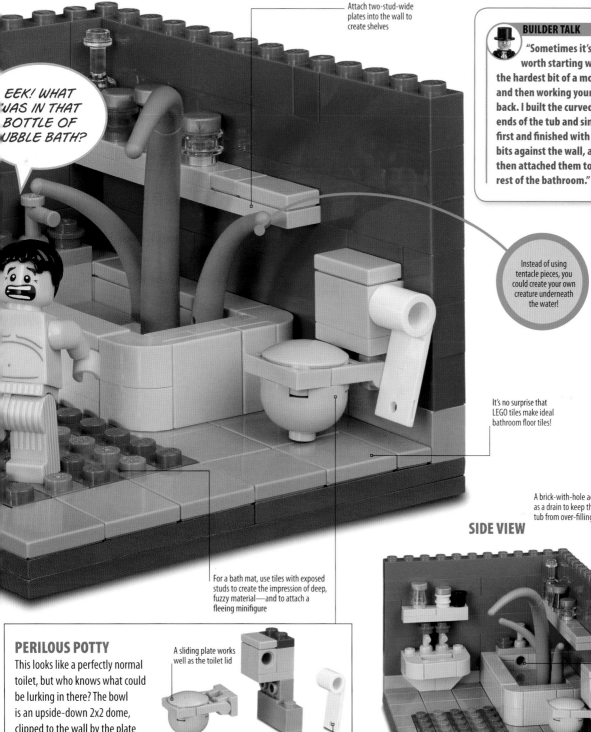

Attach two-stud-wide plates into the wall to create shelves

EEK! WHAT WAS IN THAT BOTTLE OF BUBBLE BATH?

Instead of using tentacle pieces, you could create your own creature underneath the water!

It's no surprise that LEGO tiles make ideal bathroom floor tiles!

A brick-with-hole acts as a drain to keep the tub from over-filling

SIDE VIEW

For a bath mat, use tiles with exposed studs to create the impression of deep, fuzzy material—and to attach a fleeing minifigure

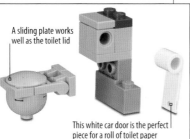

PERILOUS POTTY

This looks like a perfectly normal toilet, but who knows what could be lurking in there? The bowl is an upside-down 2x2 dome, clipped to the wall by the plate with handle above it.

A sliding plate works well as the toilet lid

This white car door is the perfect piece for a roll of toilet paper

MAD SCIENTIST'S LAB

Timmy should have heeded the warning on the sign outside, but when he sees the flashing lights and hears the weird noises from inside the lab, he can't resist taking a peek! Build a mad scientist's laboratory to conduct strange experiments in, and fill it with machines, devices, and mysterious chemicals.

ON THE SLAB
Use a 2x6 plate as the base for a monster-building operating table. A hinge placed underneath allows it to lie flat or be raised up at an angle.

Two 1x1 slopes make a cradle for the monster's head

The studs of a 1x2 plate attach to the holes in the minifigure's legs to hold it in place

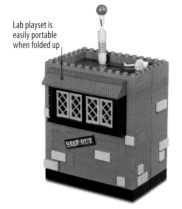

Lab playset is easily portable when folded up

FRONT SIDE VIEW

Windows let in light so the details on your model can be seen clearly

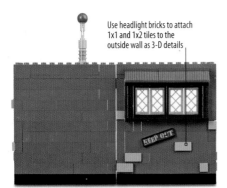

Use headlight bricks to attach 1x1 and 1x2 tiles to the outside wall as 3-D details

OPEN FRONT VIEW

MAKING SCIENCE
The mad scientist's laboratory is built as a small box that opens up to reveal a larger space for playing and storytelling. Inside are the scientist's latest projects: a pair of mechanical robots and a monster that he's bringing to life!

To find out how to build your own robots, turn to p.18

red LEGO Technic ball at
e top of a spire collects
ectricity from lightning
orms to power the mad
cientist's work

prevent the halves from
obling, place one hinge
r the bottom and
e near the top

LAB EQUIPMENT
Your lab will need equipment
to concoct all sorts of weird
and wonderful distillations.
Build pipes and tubes out
of faucets, lightsaber handles,
round bricks, LEGO Technic
T-bars, and other interestingly
shaped elements.

Only using gray pieces
makes this look like a
very complicated piece
of machinery!

FRESHLY
BREWED!

What else could you
add to your lab?
Fill the empty space
with even more
wacky equipment!

NEXT SUBJECT!
The scientist's assistant rolls in
his next experimental subject.
The trolley is a simpler version
of the operating table, with a pair
of wheels at the bottom so it can
be pushed around.

THESE TEST
SUBJECTS SURE
ARE BONE IDLE.

A plate with
handle lets a
minifigure hold
on at the top

Skeleton's feet plug
into headlight bricks

Tiles with printed gauges and dials are
very helpful for building machinery

Grille locks the headlight
bricks together

'BOTS ON THE LOOSE

Oh no! When Timmy opened the door to the lab, something got out. In fact, a whole lot of somethings did! Now his dream is full of clanking, stomping, beeping robots. When you build your own LEGO brick robots, you can make them big, small, round, square, or anything in between. Give them lots of metallic pieces and mechanical detail.

Stack a 2x2 round tile on a 2x2 round plate to make the classic stud on top of the head

Eyes are 1x1 square plates mounted on radar dishes

The head is built just like the body, only smaller

MEGA 'BOT

Do you have a favorite minifigure? Then blow it up—in scale, that is! This one is based on the Clockwork Robot. Use your bricks to construct a giant-sized version with as many of the same colors and details as possible.

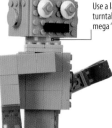

Use a large turntable for your mega 'bot's neck

Posable robotic claws are built from clips, plates with handles, sliding plates, and 1x1 slopes

SIDE VIEW

Tiles, grilles, radar dishes, and round plates recreate the original printed details on the minifigure in 3-D

Attach tiles to side studs for smooth surfaces

TITANIUM TORSO

The giant robot's torso has a core of bricks with side studs. Plates and tiles are attached to create the look of a smooth body with bolts around the chest, just like on the minifigure!

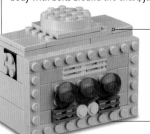

It doesn't matter what color bricks you use on the inside—they'll be hidden from view!

Feet are tipped with grille slopes

IT REALLY CAPTURES MY WINNING SMILE!

Clockwork Robot

Why not extend your 'bot family? Baby Bot might like an older brother and sister!

'BOT HEAD

To allow Mrs. Bot to turn her head, use a jumper plate with a tile on each side. Her wide jaw is made from a 2x3 curved plate with hole. Give Mrs. Bot a cute bow by attaching two 1x1 slopes.

1x1 slope

2x3 curved plate with hole

Jumper plate

Eyes are silver 1x1 round plates attached to headlight bricks

Shoulders are ray guns with their handles plugged into headlight bricks

MRS. BOT

Dark red pieces, silver accents, and lots of round elements give this robot a stylish art deco design. Her skirt is a Technic wheel element from a LEGO® *Star Wars*™ set.

A free-rotating LEGO Technic pin allows the arm to swing back and forth

Elbow is a 1x1 round tile attached to a half-pin

SIDE VIEW

FAMILY PHOTO TIME, EVERYBODY!

Grille-slope mouth creates a quirky expression

A plate with handle built into the body adds a projecting decoration

...m built out of ...GO Technic ...oss-axle ...nnectors

Upper legs are barrel-shaped droid body elements linked by a LEGO Technic pin

Each foot is made from a 1x2 plate and a 1x2 tile flipped upside down

Use 1x1 round bricks for the legs, lower arms, and parts of the torso

BABY BOT

What's the smallest robot you can build? This miniature marvel is made out of just eight pieces, starting with a brick with two side studs for its body!

Wide eyes are a binocular piece attached to a 1x1 round plate

1x1 plates with side clips make tiny arms

MR. BOT

This retro, industrial-looking robot is built mostly out of gray pieces to imitate metal. His arms swivel at the shoulders, and an unusual upside-down construction gives his feet treads.

Legs are 1x1 cones plugged into a 1x2 jumper plate

...et are inverted slopes ...ached to corrugated tubes by ...EGO Technic axle-with-stud

Grilles become treads on the bottom of the feet

ROBOT RAMPAGE

"You dare to unleash robots in MY city?" says the Inventor. "Let's see how they do against my own mechanical minions!" Suddenly there are two armies of robots battling it out in Timmy's dream. Build some 'bots that are designed for demolition and destruction! Give them claws, spikes, and any other tools they'll need to mash, smash, crunch, and munch their rivals.

Antenna picks up commands from its inventor

One-stud connections let the head and shoulders be posed

SIDE VIEW

Golden eyes plug into the bases of headlight bricks that are turned on their backs

A plate with handle creates a bar to protect the robot's head

TORNADO-TRON

This riotous red robot can spin its body around to send enemies toppling to the ground. Its boxy construction shows that it's tough and ready to rumble.

Tiles printed with dials make great robotic features

SPIN CYCLE

A 2x2 turntable in the middle of the model lets its upper body rotate freely with a flick of your finger. Or hold it by the shoulders and make its legs spin around!

2x2 turntable

Big feet keep this 'bot from toppling over

ROBOTS: ATTACK! OOPS, DID I FORGET TO BUILD AN OFF BUTTON?

A plate with side bars creates an antenna on each side of the head

Hands are 1x1 plates with horizontal clips

ZOOM-BOT

What this robot lacks in size, it makes up for with speed. Its legs are jets to rocket it around, and its claws pack an electric zap that sends bigger 'bots packing!

SIDE VIEW

Legs are 1x1 cones with round plates at the base

CHOMP CHOMP

BIT-OR

It can be fun to build a robot model around one particular feature—such as a giant set of teeth! This fellow's chompers can reduce its rivals to scrap in seconds.

Teeth are 1x4 LEGO Technic gear racks

...d plates for eyes are ...hed to headlight bricks

Hands are 1x1 plates with vertical clips

Feet are made from small LEGO Technic liftarms

HEAVY METAL

The toothy robot's limbs are sheathed in silver corrugated tubes. Thread LEGO Technic cross-axles with studs on the ends through the tubes to connect LEGO Technic pieces to regular bricks.

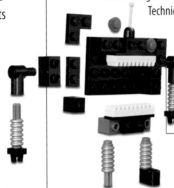

Use LEGO Technic pins to connect the arms to the body

SPI-DRONE

Not all robots have to be humanoid—let their missions determine their form. With its stealthy shape and dark color scheme, this automated arachnoid is designed to scramble across walls and ceilings as it snoops on its unwitting foes.

Insectlike limbs are robot minifigure arms with a horn plugged into the tip

A radar dish makes excellent laser-deflecting armor

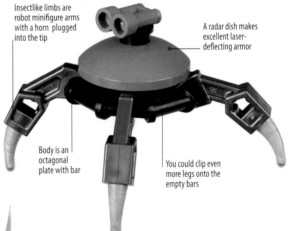

Body is an octagonal plate with bar

You could clip even more legs onto the empty bars

⭐ CHALLENGE

MINIFIGURE MEMORY

Gather a heap of your scariest minifigures and challenge your friends to a minifigure memory test! Give your friends some time to look over the minifigures, then hide them all behind a blanket and remove one. The winner is the first friend to correctly guess which minifigure is missing.

THE MUMMY'S TOMB

When Timmy calls for his mummy, this isn't what he meant. Archaeological sites are a great place to discover the past, but in the world of nightmares, they are also home to venomous snakes, moving statues, hidden traps, and pharaohs' curses!

ANCIENT RUINS

When constructing a building that is thousands of years old, don't just make clean, smooth walls. Include pieces that are rounded or textured to show its age. Off-color bricks will make it look like bits of the original stone have fallen away.

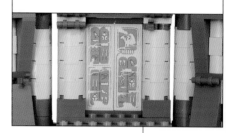

MADE OF STONE
Tall bricks with stickers from a LEGO® Pharaoh's Quest set form the heavy stone doors, but you could also build your own.

Hinges make the side walls angle in, or you could build one straight long wall

WHO DARES TO ENTER MY TOMB?

Plates with handles resemble decorative carvings

The addition of some leaves shows how nature has crept into the ruin

Scattered tan tiles on the ground give the impression of an old temple taken over by the desert

MUMMY ATTACK!

When the hidden stand behind the door bricks is pushed, the door bricks topple forward, making the lurking mummy smash through the wall!

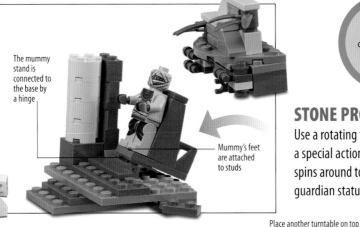

The mummy stand is connected to the base by a hinge

Mummy's feet are attached to studs

What other nightmarish creatures could be hiding in your ancient ruins?

STONE PROTECTOR

Use a rotating turntable base to create a special action function: a wall that spins around to reveal one of the tomb's guardian statues. . .or a secret treasure!

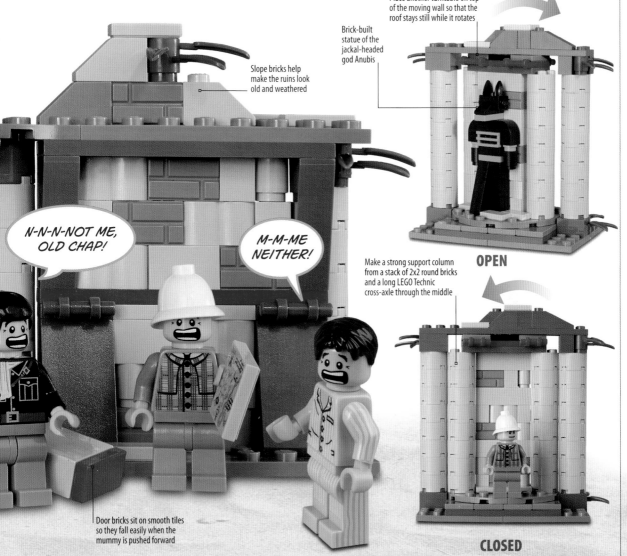

Place another turntable on top of the moving wall so that the roof stays still while it rotates

Brick-built statue of the jackal-headed god Anubis

Slope bricks help make the ruins look old and weathered

OPEN

Make a strong support column from a stack of 2x2 round bricks and a long LEGO Technic cross-axle through the middle

N-N-N-NOT ME, OLD CHAP!

M-M-ME NEITHER!

Door bricks sit on smooth tiles so they fall easily when the mummy is pushed forward

CLOSED

SKELETON

Well, that was some gratitude! As soon as Timmy finished putting the skeleton together, it started chasing him and threatening to gobble him up. It is certainly a good thing that it is all bones and no tummy. Look through your collection for long bars, curved elements, and oddly shaped pieces, and use them to build a big, scary skeleton!

BOO!

SKELETAL SPECIES

Who says this has to be a human skeleton? Make it a monster by adding horns, claws, and oversized hands and feet. Now it looks both grim and a little bit goofy—just right for a LEGO brick nightmare!

2x2 round tile for a skullcap

Brick with two holes

Horns plug into headlight bricks

NO BRAINS HERE!

The skull's eyes are a brick with two holes. For its mouth, use a transparent 1x2 plate so that the studs on the piece beneath show through as teeth.

Neck is a 1x1 cone

The center of the collarbone is a 1x1 brick with four hollow side studs

The hands are built just like the feet, but tipped with claws

A 1x2 plate with handle creates the back of the pelvis

Top of the legs are round bricks

1x1 plates with vertical clips let the arms move at the shoulder

Skeleton's ribs are minifigure skeleton arms!

The spine is a long rod piece

Hips are headlight bricks attached sideways to a brick with four side studs

Shoulder blades are 1x1 plates with side rings

Position big feet at an angle to

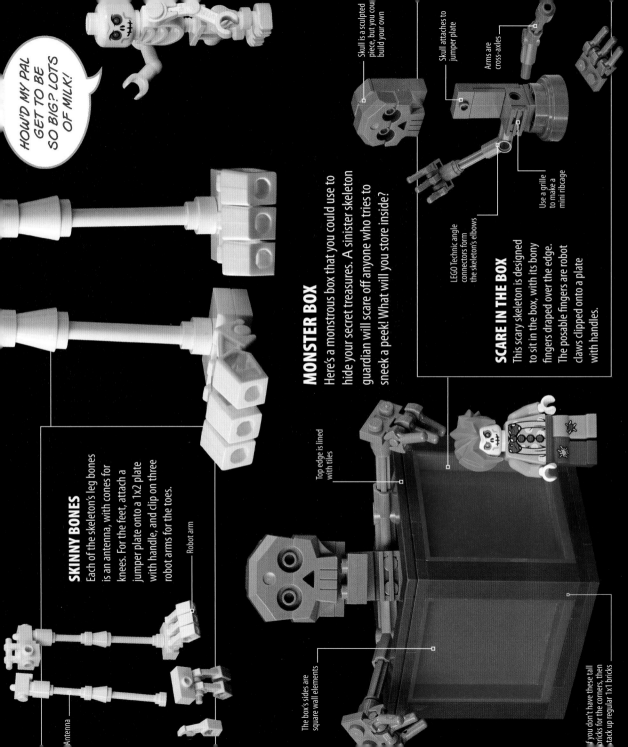

HOW'D MY PAL GET TO BE SO BIG? LOTS OF MILK!

SKINNY BONES

Each of the skeleton's leg bones is an antenna, with cones for knees. For the feet, attach a jumper plate onto a 1x2 plate with handle, and clip on three robot arms for the toes.

Robot arm

Antenna

MONSTER BOX

Here's a monstrous box that you could use to hide your secret treasures. A sinister skeleton guardian will scare off anyone who tries to sneak a peek! What will you store inside?

Skull is a sculpted piece, but you cou build your own

Skull attaches to jumper plate

Arms are cross-axles

Use a grille to make a mini ribcage

LEGO Technic angle connectors form the skeleton's elbows

SCARE IN THE BOX

This scary skeleton is designed to sit in the box, with its bony fingers draped over the edge. The posable fingers are robot claws clipped onto a plate with handles.

Top edge is lined with tiles

The box's sides are square wall elements

f you don't have these tall bricks for the corners, then tack up regular 1x1 bricks

Timmy runs away from the skeleton as fast as his little legs will carry him, until he reaches the steps of a big stone castle. "Velcome, child," he hears as the door slowly creaks open. "Von't you come in for a bite?" Vampires like to hide in castles during the day, and the older the better. Give your castle lots of classic furnishings and décor!

building castles,
but be careful not to en[d]
up with boring expanse[s]
of plain gray walls. Brea[k]
them up with multiple
windows and slopes!"

CRYPT SWEET CRYPT

Look at pictures of old castles and mansions to get ideas for your vampire's lair. For colors, use gray to resemble stone, with black and red accents. Avoid open windows—vampires aren't too fond of sunlight!

Moon (a printed glow-in-the-dark radar dish) is attached to the black rear wall using a brick with side stud

A couple of slopes can make an entire peaked rooftop

Use the backs of headlight bricks for dark, square windows

PLEASED TO EAT—I MEAN MEET YOU!

Trees are brown telescopes with upside-down flower stems on top

Pillars are plates with handles built sideways

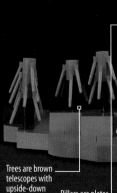

MICRO-TRANSYLVANIA

If you don't have enough pieces to make an entire vampire castle, create a micro-scale façade with your smallest LEGO pieces! Give it classic monster story details, such as a rocky mountain peak, a spooky forest, and a big full moon outside

Alternate 2x2 tiles to make a checkerboard floor pattern

COZY COFFIN

What makes a castle feel like a vampire's home? Spooky colors and details like chains and trap doors help, but a coffin for a bed really makes the model complete. If you don't have a LEGO coffin, build your own.

WINDOWS

For windows that look like they belong to a room that was built centuries ago, combine window frame pieces with latticed window elements. Surround them with gray arches and bricks to resemble stone blocks.

Arch piece fits over window frame so it can be built into a brick wall

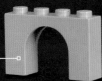

1x2 brick

Latticed window from a castle set

Make a bigger window out of sideways fence pieces and plug transparent 1x1 round plates into the gaps for a stained glass effect

A large arch creates the shape of a large window

OLD STONES

This part of the castle has been around for a long, long time. Slopes and unfinished edges make a stone wall look like it is falling apart, and textured bricks add to the appearance of decay and disrepair.

Candlestick is made from a telescope, a LEGO Technic half-pin, and a minifigure screwdriver for the wick

EEEK! EVEN I'M SCARED HERE.

Add some rodent residents to your spooky castle

Table leg attaches to the stud of a jumper plate on the floor

Combine tan and gray bricks for a weather-worn look

HANDFUL OF BRICKS LIST

4x4 plate x 1

2x2 inverted slope x 1

2x2 brick x 3

2 x 4 brick x 2

2x2 plate x 2

1x2/1x4 angle plate x1

1x6 plate x 2

2x2 slope x 3

Antenna x1

1x2 slope x 2

2x3 slope x 1

1x1 slope x 4

1x1 brick eyes x 2

1x2 tile with top bar x 1

1x2 plate x 1

1x1 round brick x 1

2x4 angled plate x 2

1x2 curved half-arch x 1

1x3 brick x 2

4x4 round plate x 1

2x2 round brick x 1

DK | Penguin Random House

For DK Publishing
Project Editor Hannah Dolan
Senior Designer Guy Harvey
Editors Jo Casey, Matt Jones, Victoria Taylor
Designers Jill Bunyan, Sam Richiardi, Lauren Rosier, Rhys Thomas
Jacket Designer David McDonald
Senior DTP Designer Kavita Varma
Pre-production Producer Siu Chan
Producer Lloyd Robertson
Managing Editor Simon Hugo
Design Manager Guy Harvey
Creative Manager Sarah Harland
Art Director Lisa Lanzarini
Publisher Julie Ferris
Publishing Director Simon Beecroft

For the LEGO Group
Project Manager Mikkel Joachim Petersen
Assistant Licensing Manager Randi Kirsten Sørensen
Senior Licensing Manager Corinna van Delden
Designer Melody Louise Caddick
Building Instruction Developer Alexandra Martin
Model makers Stephen Berry, Yvonne Doyle, Rod Gillies,
Tim Goddard, Tim Johnson, Barney Main, Pete Reid

Photography by Gary Ombler

First published in the United States in 2015 by DK Publishing
345 Hudson Street, New York, New York 10014

Contains material previously published in LEGO® *Play Book* (2013)

001—284611—Mar/15

Page design copyright © 2015 Dorling Kindersley Limited.
A Penguin Random House Company.

Acknowledgments
Dorling Kindersley would like to thank: Randi Sørensen, Mikkel Petersen,
Melody Caddick, Corinna van Delden, and Alexandra Martin at the LEGO Group;
Stephen Berry, Yvonne Doyle, Rod Gillies, Tim Goddard, Tim Johnson, Barney Main,
Pete Reid, and Andrew Walker for their amazing models; Daniel Lipkowitz for his inspiring
text; Gary Ombler for his endless patience and brilliant photography; and Emma Grange,
Lauren Nesworthy, Lisa Stock, and Matt Wilson for editorial and design assistance.

A WORLD OF IDEAS:
SEE ALL THERE IS TO KNOW

1x1 brick x 7

4x6 plate

1x1 headlight brick x 2

1x4 brick

1x2 brick x 5
(including 1 transparent)

1x6 brick

2x3 brick

1x2 jumper plate x 3

1x2x1 panel

1x1 round plate x 2

1x4 plate

2x2 radar dish x 2

Wide rim, wide tire
and 2x2 axle plate
with 1 pin

1x1 cone x 1

2x6 plate x 3

1x1 plate

1x2 grille plate x 2

2x4 plate

Faucet x 1

1x6 arch brick

2x2 round plate x 2

4x4 radar dish